EASTLEIGH

The Railway · The Town · The People

Bob Winkworth

Dedication

To my Grandfather, and also to
my wife, Brenda – for help and
encouragement.

N.B.

EASTLEIGH CARR WORKS
TRAVELLING STEAM CRANE

EASTLEIGH

The Railway · The Town · The People

Bob Winkworth

ISBN (10) 0 –9554110-0-9
(13) 978-0-9554110-0-7

First published in 2007 by Kevin Robertson
under the **NOODLE BOOKS** imprint
PO Box 279
SOUTHAMPTON
SO32 3ZX

www.noodle.books@tesco.net

Printed in England by
The Amadeus Press
Cleckheaton
West Yorkshire

Front cover - top: **Platform 4 – the Portsmouth Loop 1931**. Either a Waterloo to Southampton Terminus service via Alton, or an Eastleigh to Fareham and Gosport train, waiting at Platform 4 on Tuesday 8th September. The engine is a rebuilt Drummond 4-6-0 No 459 of the 'T14' class. Due to their original appearance, these were appropriately named 'Paddleboxes', and even after rebuilding in the form seen here the nickname still stuck.. Never a particularly successful design, this type of secondary route service was typical of the duties they performed.

Front cover - lower: **Corner of Newtown Road and George Street - 1.** Messrs Knight were known to have occupied these premises from at least 1926 although the Ford van suggests an earlier date. The display includes the usual variety of enamel signs and the almost obligatory Cadbury's window advert.

Rear cover: **Station Front.** Hemmed in as it was by railway on three sides, public access to the station was from Southampton Road and with Leigh Road – from where this view was taken - immediately opposite. The lime trees on the pavement were a feature of several Eastleigh streets and whilst development and changes have taken place on the left, beneath a veneer of more modern fascias and awnings, many of the remaining buildings in this view still survive in these early years of the 21st century.

Preceding pages: **Carriage Works Steam Crane.** An unusual vehicle recorded during what is probably some time in the first two decades of the twentieth century. The origins of this crane are unknown and whilst the main components were undoubtedly provided by an outside contractor, the cab and roof must have been home made. The legend on the card referring to the capacity meant this vehicle could no doubt be used to lift vehicle bogies and the ends of vehicle under-frames but it would have been too weak to lift a complete wagon or coach.

Introduction

I suppose there has always been 'steam', running through my veins as both my grandfathers and one great grandfather had moved to Eastleigh Works from Nine Elms in 1910. Indeed my maternal grandad was one of the first to move into what were then the new railway houses in Campbell Road. These were considered luxurious for the time although later on the nick-name of 'Spike Island' would be applied to the same dwellings, a cruel reference to the fact that Campbell Road was hemmed in by railway lines on every side.

One of my grandfathers was also involved in the installation of some of the machinery in what was then the new works, and in particular the steam driven pulley and belt system through which all the works machinery was then powered. With the works eventually in full production grandfather himself would later be employed in the erecting shop. My father subsequently followed him, being employed in the boiler shop operating the ride-on planing machine, and later in the machine shop operating a milling machine.

Other family members – not all resident in Eastleigh - worked in other parts of the locomotive and carriage works, including the carriage paint shop. With such connections then steam could be indeed be said to have become an intrinsic part of me.

However, when it did eventually come to my own time for employment, perhaps that very steam in my body was not quite superheated enough, for my own career moved in other directions, although the love of railways and local history has persisted from my earliest recollections through to today.

The closest then I would come to the works areas was on what were for many years the regular open-days, usually held on a Saturday in August and including a fete held on a stretch of grass between the front of the works and the line from Eastleigh to Portsmouth. (Yes…like Crewe, Eastleigh still retained some greenery despite the presence of the works).

To an impressionable youngster these open days – and the other visits I made to the works at other times - provide an enduring memory. In the works themselves I would walk through showers of sparks in the welding shop, get near deafened in the boiler shop and watch spellbound as a pair of huge driving wheels swung effortlessly through empty space above my head in the erecting shop. Then there was the thump of mighty drop hammers in the forge, hammers which could be controlled almost with a feather light touch when needed. All of this contrasting with the relative peace to be found in the moulding, pattern making and paint shops.

Outside I would collect numbers from the many locomotives both on display and in the scrap roads. Then, filthy dirty, it was home on the works bus with Dad and a scrub in the sink…

I could not have envisioned at the time that what I was seeing would eventually lead to the steady acquisition and collation of railway post-card views of Eastleigh around what were the halcyon days of the works, and by this I refer to the period from around 1900 to perhaps 1939.

The railway was then easily the biggest employer in the town and, as such, much of the municipal area was tied up with railway connections. Fetes, marches, schools - all were provided either by or for railway staff and their families and it is these aspects of the social history as well as the railway history of the borough that I have attempted both to collate and also to record in the following pages.

Many of the scenes thus recorded would have been commonplace to my grandparents: indeed the infrastructure remained much the same into the late 1960s. But not so nowadays. For 2005 saw the end of Eastleigh as a major railway maintenance facility, with the construction of both locomotives and rolling stock having already ceased many years earlier.

The views captured in the photographs that follow are impossible to repeat, and afford a unique insight into a time when Eastleigh was both a proud railway town and an area of individual character. A period of time in which, over a few short decades, character, interest, and industry flourished.

Bob Winkworth.
Eastleigh 2006.

THE INSTITUTE, EASTLEIGH.

3258

Above: **The Railway in the Community**. Aside from affording a means of transport previously inaccessible to the public at large, the advent of the railway also meant mass employment for the Eastleigh area. In addition, and away from the public arena, most of the towns with large railway workshops erected institutes – as well as other socially minded buildings - for the benefit of the staff. The Railway Institute at Eastleigh was erected in 1891 and stood on the corner of Leigh Road and Market Street and in the location now occupied by Sainsbury's supermarket. It survived just over 90 years and was demolished in 1982.

Opposite page - top: **Men-only Outing from the Railway Institute circa 1920**. Members of the Railway Institute came from all grades of worker, and they would regularly arrange outings – Whitsun Bank Holiday was a favourite - perhaps surprisingly using motor rather than rail transport. The charabanc in view is a solid tyre AEC, reportedly one of three being used on this occasion (early 1920s) for this particular outing. This actual vehicle was operated by 'Royal Blue'. The destination for the day was not recorded although, bearing in mind the limitations of the road network as well as the comfort of the vehicle, something like a 30 to 40 mile radius was probably the practical maximum. Indeed it is known that the New Forest and River Thames were favoured spots – not on the same day of course. Of the 26 men visible, including the driver, only one is without any form of headgear.

Opposite page - lower: **William Adams 'T1' Class 0-4-0T No 62 from Campbell Road Bridge.** Recorded in June 1924, the engine is No 62 and from the head-code is probably that of a local between Southampton Terminus and Eastleigh or Basingstoke. Beyond the vans and standing on what was the siding of the Outdoor Machinery Section (now a motorcycle dealer) is a small group of railway cottages, the physically bigger size of these compared with the terrace dwellings fronting Southampton Road meaning that the former were probably occupied by supervisory grades. All of the remaining dwellings to the east of the roadway have since been demolished and the site is now occupied by a car park, various industrial units, and a filling station. To the left is the exit road from the locomotive shed, with the connection affording direct access to the main down line. Although remaining in situ for many years, it does not appear even at this early stage that this connection was much used. (H.C. Casserley)

Above: **Memorial Plaque within the Railway Works**. Forty two men from the LSWR Works at Eastleigh lost their lives during the Great War; this was one of the two memorials erected to their memory. Since the rundown and closure of the site the whereabouts of these memorials is unknown.

Opposite page - top: **'Engine after Collision at Eastleigh, April 30th 1908'.** Tantalisingly, further details of the incident referred to are not given, although close inspection reveals the buffer beam and running plate to be bent backwards. Superficially at least then relatively minor damage. This was also only five days after the great snowfall (see later) and so it is tempting to suggest the two events *could* perhaps be linked. The engine is of course a 'K10' 4-4-0, No 340, also being referred to as a 'Small Hopper', and the container on the side of the firebox is seen fitted with firebox cross tubes.

Opposite page - lower: **Charity Auction within the Carriage and Wagon Works.** Despite having existed on the site for upwards of 70 years, views of any type from *within* the Carriage and Wagon works are rare. This particular scene dates from 1918 and records the forthcoming auction of garden produce in aid of the St Dunstan's Hostel for blind serviceman. Aside from the male workers, it is also possible to discern at least two women on the right hand side – there were no doubt others employed in the works as well. The use made of natural light both here and within the nearby locomotive works is very apparent.

ENGINE. AFTER. COLLISION. AT. EASTLEIGH. APRIL 30. '08.

Returning to Works, L.S.W Ry, Eastleigh, Hants.   5357.

This page, above and overleaf: **Work in progress building 'The Works'** The framework for the new locomotive works in place in 1905. Construction methods would appear to have been similar to those of today, with a steel framework in between which was brick infill. What can be clearly seen as well is that construction was on previously virgin land.

Opposite page -top: **Carriage Works Staff.** The view is of present day Bishopstoke Road and looking up the slope towards the railway bridge. On the left is one of the access routes to the actual Carriage and Wagon Works whilst on the right is the now long demolished Carriage Works canteen. There would have been little chance of any vehicle making a successful headway against such a throng – fortunately the age of the motor car was still some time away.

'Opposite page -lower: **Band of Hope' Parade.** From the same location the Wesleyan 'Band of Hope' parade is seen making its way to The Mount at Bishopstoke where the annual meeting was held. It can be seen that the card is dated Saturday 6th July 1907, and with the local photographer responsible for it, he was certainly quick off the mark as the postmark was that of just eight days later in Guildford.

Above: **The Front of the Works Yard - 1.** A panoramic view of the front of the works yard around 1910, with a variety of the products of Messrs. Beattie, Adams, and Drummond on view together with numerous locomotive tenders and what were probably goods vehicles used for bringing in or removing components. The view could well have been recorded on a Sunday as there does not appear to be a single person present. Ironically, and despite this clearly being a South Western related scene, the actual postcard was sent to a London address and referred to a hoped for social meeting at Euston station! The postmark itself is somewhat smudged although the sending date of December 19th 1910 is clear.

Opposite page - top: **The Front of the Works Yard - 2.** Still displaying its newly built appearance but with a few additions outside as well. The bland façade gives little clue as to what might be taking place inside, although disgorged into the sunlight on the left are at least two locomotives fresh from overhaul. At least one of these may well be an Adams 4-4-0. A Drummond '700' class 0-6-0 is also visible. The presence of the wooden post - obviously not a signal, but complete with turned finial is curious.

Opposite page - lower: **The Locomotive Works Offices - 1.37 pm.** Depicted when probably brand new in 1908/9, the main offices for the works stood on the west of the site and fronted both the running sheds' arrival and departure roads as well as the main running lines. Part of the front of the works can just be seen in the right background. The structure remained in use as offices throughout the duration of the site as a workshop and was little altered. In the foreground the dead-end siding is of interest and is believed to have been a short lived facility used during the construction of the building

1424 L. & S. W. R. Works, Eastleigh.

Turn out at the Loco Works. This was purchased as a wash painted coloured card showing turnout at the Loco Works at the end of the shift. The view is supposedly dated 1924, but the scene would have been typical of that pervading for years previous as well. Whilst on the original card the colour wash has perhaps reduced the detail slightly, the result in so far as the workers seen, is to record them almost in the style of the great L S Lowry, with matchstick style figures.

Loco Works Gate No 1. This particular works access was located on the end of Campbell Road Bridge, with the building at the bottom of the steps being the timekeeper's office. Immediately to the right is the loco Works Canteen. The loco works hooter would sound to indicate to all the time of the lunchtime break - as here, and then also at the end of the working day.

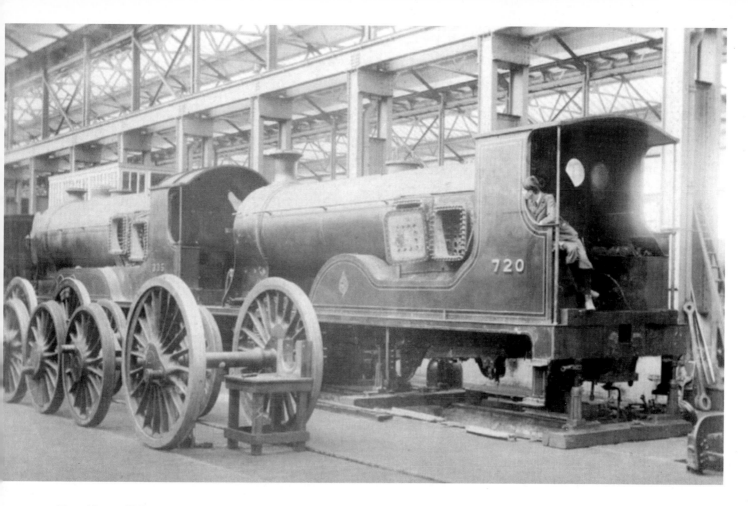

Two 'One-off' Drummond Designs inside the Works. Nearest the camera, No 720 was a 4-2-2-0 design built in 1897 and originally coupled to a tender fitted with a water scoop although, as such facilities were never provided on any South Western lines, the scoop was later removed. After a lacklustre career No 720 was withdrawn in 1927. In front is 'E14' class 4-6-0 No 335. Built in 1907 it too was a poor performer to start with, but was improved somewhat after rebuilding as an 'H15' by Robert Urie in 1914. It would survive as BR No 30335 until 1959. The person in the cab of No 720 is certainly not a workshop man and could well be a visitor.

The Boiler Shop.
Without doubt the noisiest place within the works was the boiler shop due to the cacophony of sound emanating from the riveting guns. A man who worked here throughout his life was almost certain to end up deaf, yet such a risk was accepted as normal. Small wonder then that communication between the men here was only possible through sign language and lip reading.

Erecting Shop

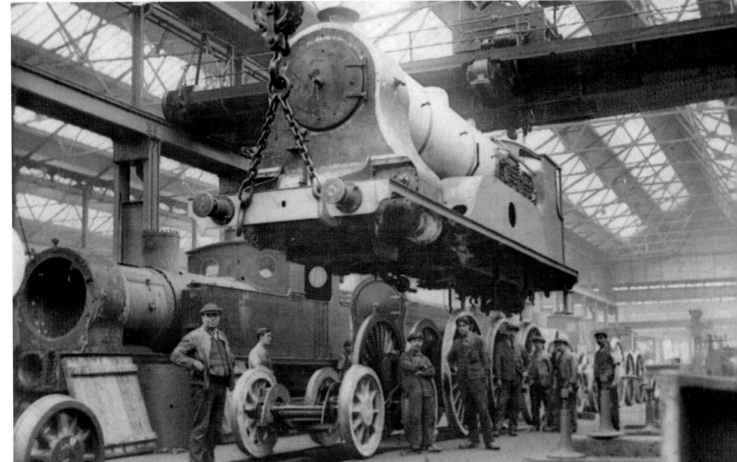

ERECTING SHOP. LOCO. WORKS. EASTLEIGH. R.B. S. No. 2.

Above: The Erecting Shop - 1. Work in progress on 'H15' class 4-6-0, the wheels for which have yet to be added. The date then must be sometime between 1914 and 1925. Seven men are visible, possibly forming one particular gang and who would each be paid a bonus according to the efficiency of the group as a whole

Opposite page - top: The Erecting Shop - 2. 'D15' 4-4-0 No 467 aloft in the Erecting Shop possibly even around the time of its build in 1912. Clearly a posed view, the impression given is one of order and organisation with walkways kept clear and respective components alongside the various engines. Something that was lacking at Eastleigh in this view though is that of a hand operated trolley way between the rails which was provided at a number of other companys' sites. No 467 worked until 1955

Opposite page - lower: The Erecting Shop - 3. What may well be a brand new 'T14' in the final stages of building, possibly then around 1911. The same shop of course was used for both new building and repairs – as witness the 'O2' 0-4-4T No 232 on the left. The 'T14' will now be carefully lowered onto its wheels, one man at the position of each axlebox and each ready to ensure these items line up within the frames. Following this the springs and motion will be added.

Erecting Shop Workers 1937. Seven men forming the Frame Gang within the Erecting Shop, some of whose names are recorded. Left to right they are: Jack Ridge – grandfather to the author; Harry Page; unknown: ? Evans - with hammer; standing; 'Tadpole' Bigley; Jack Emery, and finally on the extreme right a very youthful Harry Frith. Harry Frith remained at Eastleigh throughout his working life and was Erecting Shop foreman in the final days of steam. He later went on to advise the Eastleigh Preservation Society on the restoration of 'S15' 4-6-0 No 828. The men are next to the frames of a 'T9'.

Surviving LSWR Signals – August 1950. The lattice bracket carrying the up main home signals for Eastleigh East box and the corresponding distant signals for the West box. This particular signal was located just north of Campbell Road overbridge, hence the need for height and also the provision of the co-acting repeater arms beneath. In the background are the carriage sidings as well as the roof of the carriage works. The signals in the 'off' position indicate 'all clear' on the up through line.

Front End of the Running Sheds. Recorded from the vicinity of the main line to Southampton, this is the front end of the running sheds with the offices, water tower and coaling stage on the left. In addition to housing the office block, the tall building also afforded an enginemen's dormitory, at a time when lodging terms for footplate staff were commonplace. Even so, because of the location,this must have been a recipe for many a sleepless night – or day. Missing from the view is the eye-sight signal which was later fixed high up on the corner of the office block. As the name would imply this was used as a means of assessing a footplateman's eyesight. The water tank was fed directly from the River Itchen and it was stated that when occasionally cleaned out, considerable quantities of fish would be found. The running sheds had been moved from Northam in 1903.

Above: **The Rear of the Running Shed.** What is probably a 1920s or early 1930s view of the depot, with the products of Messrs Adams, Drummond, and Urie in view. Already the ravages of time are taking their toll with missing panes of glass evident. Notice though the modern form of yard lighting – electricity. On the extreme left is the end of the shed offices which extended along much of the south side.

Opposite page - top: **Inside the Running Shed - 1**. The running sheds, also referred to as the 'Locomotive Cleaning Sheds' in contemporary literature, and which had been established in 1903, replaced a smaller two road shed on the same site. This previous building had itself superseded an earlier locomotive depot north of the station and in the area of the Salisbury branch junction. Depicted inside the depot on Thursday 16th July 1925 is 'T1' 0-4-4T No 358 and also '460' class 4-4-0 No 474.

Opposite page - lower: **Inside the Running Shed - 2.** The shed provided covered accommodation over no less than 15 roads together with a small one road repair road and wheel lift on the south side. As was typical for the period, wooden smoke troughs were provided. In addition to attempting to maximise the use of natural light, glass was also prevalent. In view of the presence of gas lighting allied to the steam engines themselves, it is perhaps surprising that there were not more instances of fires within the structures of similar buildings. The two nearest locomotives are Adams Jubilee type, No 544, and No 598.

592. EASTLEIGH

MENTOR & Co.
SOUTHAMPTON

(WEST END) EASTLEIGH STATION. S.W.R.

Above: **Eastleigh – West End**. LSWR practice was to refer to the junctions at Eastleigh according to the geographical position relative to London rather than their true compass locations. In terms of railway vocabulary this was   in the left background, despite being located at the south end of the complex. The view is towards the station, again from Campbell Road Bridge, sometime between 1903 and 1908, and prior to the works offices being constructed. The train of wagons awaiting exit from the loco shed road is interesting and could well be coal empties.

Opposite page - top: **From Campbell Road Bridge - posted on 24th January 1912.** The vantage point of Campbell Road Bridge has already been referred to, and here is another example of the wonderful view it afforded. The signal gantry of course predates that seen in the earlier view, and there is also plenty of activity with three locos awaiting to exit to their various duties and two arriving to go on shed. Further locomotives and rolling stock are visible in the background. A final point of interest is the magnificent telegraph pole , possessing at least 15 arms.

Opposite page - lower: **Southampton Service Departing.** Although somewhat faded this is a similar view to the previous one, but also shows the slope leading up to the Campbell Road Bridge from Southampton Road. The train, a main line service and probably hauled by an Adams or Dubbs 4-4-2T, is running on the down line. The origins of the name given to Campbell Road are interesting in themselves, and it may well be reasonable to suggest this was in some way connected with Dugald Drummond who was the Chief Mechanical Engineer of the LSWR at the time both the works and running shed were conceived. As the name would imply, he also clearly hailed from Scotland. On this occasion the posting date of the card was 15th March 1907.

PAINT SHOP. LOCO. WORKS. EASTLEIGH. R.B. S No. II.

Above: **The Paint Shop - 2**. Locomotives receiving what were almost the finishing touches inside the paint shop possibly in the last days of the LSWR. This particular part of the works was alongside north wall. Interestingly it appears that possibly all the machines on view (a Drummond 'D15', Adams '0395', a 'K10' and an 'L12') have their front cylinder covers missing.

Opposite page - top: **The Paint shop – 1.** Nine Elms-built Adams 'X2' 4-4-0 in the Eastleigh paint shop, no doubt following overhaul. The standard of craftsmanship in the finish applied was typical of the period, the overall standard of cleanliness also allowing the works number '588' to be read on the rear of the tender in front.

Opposite page - lower: **The Works 'Dump'.** A melancholy scene at the works scrap yard – also known as 'The Dump' during the 1930s. Long lines of displaced Stroudley tank engines await their fate together with at least two Adams 'Jubilee' class engines. Some have already been cannibalised, as witness No 2233 in the foreground which is devoid of its centre pair of driving wheels. A reprieve though would occur for both No 2233 and its neighbour No 2232 as both would be destined to survive - on paper at least - until the summer of 1946.

APRIL 25 1908

APRIL 25 1908

Above: **Freak April Blizzards – 1.** Saturday 25ᵗʰ April 1908 saw freak blizzards affecting southern Hampshire and the Isle of Wight. Not surprisingly the railways were severely affected, this the scene at what was for many years Platform 4 (used for Gosport and Portsmouth line services) with a few workmen having what would appear to be an insurmountable task in attempting to deal with the effects of nature through muscle power alone.

Opposite page - lower: **Freak April Blizzards – 2.** The scene at the south end of the station which was equally badly affected. The silhouetted man in the foreground could well be considering just what possibly can be done. In the background is what may well be a reboilered Adams class '460' 4-4-0, standing alongside Eastleigh West signal box. Outside the railway perimeter the large building was part of the Fair Oak Dairy. [Further south in the Solent the weather was also responsible for a tragic collision between two ships with much loss of life.

This page: **Freak April Blizzards – 3**. Winter chills, and with what appears to be a cold railway guard - judging by his having his hands in his pockets - in conversation with a somewhat warmer man in charge of a broom. With the church in the background it is easy to locate the view as being in Leigh Road and with the recreation ground behind the fence.

APRIL 25 1908

Freak April Blizzards - 4. Erected in 1894, the prominent Eagle Buildings in Leigh Road area is viewed, the outer wings of which were still extant in 2006. Messrs Woolworths can be identified, and is almost the only retailer still present today. Other premises contemporary on the site at the time were R Fletcher – Butcher; Caseys - Florist; Lloyds Bank, and The Railway Institute.

STATION FRONT.

Freak April Blizzards – 5. An interesting view of how Southampton Road alongside the station was affected and with its deserted appearance, it would seem that most people sensibly remained indoors at this time. Some effort appears to have made to clear at least part of the roadway although it is not unreasonable to assume that the council was as equally poorly prepared for the downfall as was the railway.

APRIL 25 1908

Freak April Blizzards - 6. Market Street and looking south after the snowstorm. The effect on the railway has already been depicted and fortunately the photographer took the opportunity to record the disruption elsewhere. The building on the left is on the site of what is now Regal Buildings – it was then a newsagent. On the left the advertisements are for postcards and stationary. The confectioner's (second on the left) was for many years a bakers, where the writer recalls buying 1d buns – after the 6d rush at the cinema on Saturday morning. The first floor level of many of these buildings remain little altered up to the present day. Ironically the same year that saw the snowstorm experienced a very hot summer.

Freak April Blizzards - 7. This time the view is looking north along Market Street and with the premises of Messrs John Groves, wine merchants visible. Assuming the clock was working, the time of the incident is also nicely recorded for posterity. The prominent building in the right distance was the original site for Lloyds Bank – since relocated. Also visible at left was Baker's Outfitters, more recently a chemist. The tower was subsequently demolished.

Freak April Blizzards - 8. A little further south and we witness the man on the left struggling with a handcart belonging to the London Central Meat Co. Note the gas lighting outside of Earthorne's Outfitters and also the Oliver's shoe shop. The latter firm lasted until comparatively recently. Beyond the end of the block is what is now part of The Swan Centre and Tesco.

Freak April Blizzards – 9, and Forgotten Shops and Businesses. Before the times of national and even global ownership of business, numerous small traders occupied individual shops both in Eastleigh and elsewhere. Here in this view of what was then the High Street by its junction with Factory Road, are a number of long gone businesses, including to the right a retail outlet for Scrase Brewery, the parent company of which was based in Southampton. Adjacent are Dear Bros – Bacons Factors, Framptons, and then the London Meat Supply Stores. The whole area is now part of The Swan Centre.

MARKET STREET EASTLEIGH, 4.P.M. JULY 27TH 1905.

PHOTO BY R.C.CLENCH

Above: **More Weather Problems.** This time the date is 27th July 1905. The large building on the right was Butler's Ironmongers and which stood at the junction with Blenheim Road.

Opposite page - top: **Children from Derby Road Council School**. Believed to date from around 1910 and around the time the school was built. Notice all the children are wearing a form of bow with a small bell on a ribbon across the ends. It is possible the actual view, whilst showing pupils from the school, may not have been recorded at the actual location.

Opposite page - lower: **Casualty Clearing Hospital – 1.** The RAMC (Royal Army Medical Corps) Regimental Band photographed outside the school and with a limited array of instruments.

Above: **Casualty Clearing Hospital – 2.** In this view all of the cooking and messing facilities have been laid outside and with the serving tables and containers in the foreground. Chamberlayne Road was also the first school attended by the author in 1947. The school itself was been built in 1897.

Above: **Casualty Clearing Hospital – 3.** One of a number of temporary hospital facilities in the area in use from about 1915 onwards. This particular site was adjacent to Chamberlayne Road Boys School and with the typical temporary huts of the period. This particular facility was open from July 1915 through to May 1919. Another hospital of similar type was located on the Eastleigh Recreation Ground around this time.

Opposite page - top: **Casualty Clearing Hospital – 4.** A good view of the rows of huts with soldiers being treated by RAMC staff for a variety of wounds. In the background are some of the houses in Cranbury Road.

Opposite page - lower: **Casualty Clearing Hospital – 5.** The former boys' school hall with all the beds set out for the wounded soldiers. The hall is just as recalled by the author these decades later, with classrooms set off on both sides of the hall.

Eastleigh Variety Theatre. The foundation stone for the theatre was laid in 1910 and it opened the following year on 5th June 1911. From the number assembled, it may be that some of the children are from a show being performed at the time. Photographed in October 1917, the onlookers are probably from one of the First World War clearing hospitals in the area, and include a Padre standing towards the girls' right. Adult admission charges around this time were 3d, 6d, and 9d, with children at half-price. This was against an average railway worker's wage of £1, 3s weekly.

Inset: **Children's Fancy Dress**. A group either ready for a fancy dress parade or possibly even the carnival. From the costumes an amazing amount of variety and ingenuity can be seen, particularly those of the scarecrow and Spanish lady.

6.45 EASTL

Above: **An Unusual Visitor.** A former GWR twin diesel car set but seen strengthened with an unmatched third car, passing through Eastleigh southbound on an unrecorded date. The railwayman on the opposite platform appears to have been caught on the hop! Regretfully no details are known of this run, but it was most likely to have been a possible test to ascertain the suitability of using these types of vehicles on services off the Western Region. If so such a plan did not develop further.

Opposite page - top: **Platform 1 – the Salisbury Loop.** Used mainly by Portsmouth to Salisbury (via Chandlers Ford) trains, Platform 1 was, due to its curvature, also restricted to certain classes of engine. Clearly such a restriction did not apply to 'K10' No 388, which is sporting a rather ungainly Urie pattern chimney, and was indeed recorded on a stopping Salisbury line service. Headcodes would also usually apply to the same services regardless of direction of travel. [The reference 's28' referred to the loco duty number]. To the right the rear of the building was part of the Junction Hotel.

Opposite page - lower: **Platform 4 in Normal Times.** 'T1' class 0-4-4 as Southern Railway No 3 'waiting for the road' at Platform 4 on 11th August 1938. Members of the 'T1' class were associated with the Eastleigh area throughout the whole life of the class, with the last examples being withdrawn shortly after nationalisation. None therefore received actual 30000 numbers although on paper at least, these have been allotted.

Above: **Main Line Platforms.** Viewed north through the station just as a Drummond designed 'L11' No 406 arrives at Platform 3. The headcode carried by the engine is interesting and could well relate to a special train judging by the amount of luggage seen. The structural design of the buildings on what was then designated Platform 2, to the left, has changed little over the ensuing decades.

Opposite page - top: **Mixing Southern and Great Western.** Drummond built 'L11' class 4-4-0 No 439 on Swindon built coaches and with what may well be an excursion to Southampton Docks. Part of the posts from the very tall up line signals can be seen – located at this height so that drivers of up trains could identify their position on the approach to the station. Beyond are the Bishopstoke Road Bridge and the 'East' signal cabin. The view was taken in the final peaceful days of summer on 30th July 1939.

Opposite page - lower: **Show Event.** A float decorated for a 1909 Eastleigh show and obviously prepared by the Wheel Shop. Possibly this event predated and developed into what would later be the Eastleigh Carnival. The float itself is of interest as it is could well be that the wheels are wooden patterns. Likewise…is it a rail-borne trolley that the items are standing upon? Finally, and unrelated, notice the works plate just visible on the Campbell Road side of the running shed water tower. This depicted the maker as the 'LSWR Wimbledon Works'.

Steak at 7d- 8d per Pound. The Imperial Meat Co. from High Street in 1912 and selling what was then expensive steak. The display shows meat from prize-winning beef stock supplied by W. A. Brown of Hill Lane, Southampton, later to become the 'Brown' in Brown and Harrison Dairies.

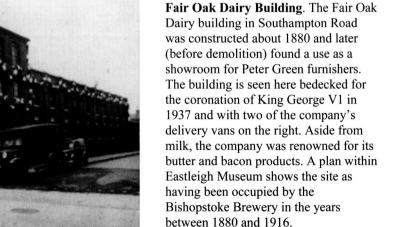

Fair Oak Dairy Building. The Fair Oak Dairy building in Southampton Road was constructed about 1880 and later (before demolition) found a use as a showroom for Peter Green furnishers. The building is seen here bedecked for the coronation of King George V1 in 1937 and with two of the company's delivery vans on the right. Aside from milk, the company was renowned for its butter and bacon products. A plan within Eastleigh Museum shows the site as having been occupied by the Bishopstoke Brewery in the years between 1880 and 1916.

Jubilee Sale Time. Baker's outfitters in Leigh Road and at the time of their Jubilee promotion of 1935. [The celebration was that of 25 years on the throne for King George V.] Clearly the discount being offered – 3/- in the pound and equivalent to 15% - was enough to attract a large crowd of prospective bargain hunters. Baker's had first opened in 1893 although the same premises has been a chemist now for many years.

MARKET STREET, EASTLEIGH.

All Quiet on the Home Front. Looking along Market Street in December 1940 with a 'Home and Colonial' delivery tricycle to the left. In the background is the Picture House Cinema opposite which was another cinema, The Regal. The prominent building located in the middle right background was Lloyds Bank while on the right is Dibben's Hardware Stores. (The same store is shown elsewhere with staff outside.)

Opposite the 'Rec'. Garton's Stationary Stores in Leigh Road opposite the Recreation Ground. Aside from stationary supplies the firm also dealt in picture postcards. To the right is the well known local photographer, Alfred Webb. The extended shop-fronts visible were eventually removed to allow for pavement widening.

Derby Road – Market Street Post Office. The former Hockey's Post office and Grocery Store taken between 1901 and 1910. After closure of the original business it became a joke and party materials shop, but at the time of writing now stands empty.

SOUTHAMPTON. R^d

Nº 2.

Market Street, Eastleigh.

Above: Essential Shopping. The tobacconist opposite the station entrance and alongside The Home Tavern – this latter building at least still exists even if in different guise. This of course was during the period unlike the present day, when smoking was socially acceptable, and indeed the vast majority of working men were smokers. Within the doorway stands a man who may well be the proprietor - and he is of course smoking himself. The shop was demolished as early as 1911, in connection with the widening of Leigh Road.

Opposite page - top: Houses for the Workers -1. Built originally as accommodation for Shop Foreman and men of similar grade, these particular properties were located in Southampton Road which was at one time known as Wide Lane along almost of its length. (Lesser grades occupied properties without the benefit of bay windows). Julian's Grocery Store is on the left and was typical of the corner shops that abounded at the end of the roads forming the grid iron concept of railway houses originally built. As an example of the expansion of the borough, the population grew from just 200 in 1850 to 1200 by 1889.

Opposite page - lower: Market Street - 1906. Contemporary in so far as the roof line of the buildings of a century ago is still recognisable today, this view depicts the Eastleigh Variety Theatre, and the wonderfully named 'Hygienic Machine Bakery' and Tea Rooms.

'Pity the Task of the Stock Taker'. Another ironmongers and with what can only be described as a nightmare for the stock taker on view. On the right is a large stock of tools, with saws and axes from 1/- to 10/-, and also all manner of brushes and fencing. To the left are household items, including cutlery, washing bowls, breadbins and so on. W.M. Dibben later moved to Southampton Road as a builders' merchants as well as having branches in other towns.

FURNISHING
IRONMONGER   60

MARMALADE MACHINES
ON

BLENHEIM. ROAD. EASTLEIGH.

Above: **Lyric Laundry Float.** Believed to date from 1910, the crown on the front suggests this could be a celebration for the coronation of King George V.   The actual laundry was situated at 120 Southampton Road, with a Mrs Funnell listed in contemporary street directories as the proprietor. The cart was probably provided by another local business, Goodenough's, which was located next to the laundry.

Opposite page - top: **Variety of Goods**. Butler's 'Ironmongery' with an amazing variety of wares available. The actual building, by then Marsh's Stores, was destroyed by fire in 1909.

Opposite page - lower: **Corner of Newtown Road and George Street –2.** By 1931 the same premises as depicted on the cover were occupied by Messrs James although the adverts appear unaltered. In view are Mrs James and her daughter Evelyn.

Above: **Steam Wagon**. Little is known of this interesting view of a steam wagon or its load photographed by the Church of the Resurrection, also known as the Parish Church. What is known is that the vehicle was owned by George Baker & Sons of Southampton and with the registration either 'MI' or 'ME' 9126. Was this an early relation to what was later Baker's Transport of Southampton?

Opposite page - top: **Gough's Butchers.** A short lived trader, probably from around 1907 to 1915 only, Gough's Butchers premises were in Leigh Road.

Opposite page - lower: **Individual Travel**. A very smart horse drawn phaeton outside the original Town Hall in Leigh Road although unfortunately undated

SOUTHAMPTON, ROAD.   120

Above: **Southampton Road - 1907.** Viewed towards the station and with two men possibly going 'on duty'. On the left, mid distance, can be seen the original Eastleigh Police House and prior to this being relocated in Leigh Road. Also visible is more of the Fair Oak Dairy site, which was referred to earlier. Notice also the extensive signal gantry visible at the south (west) end of the station. Unlike its neighbour, Southampton, Eastleigh never possessed a tramway network. Until 1924, Eastleigh Police Station was located to the left of where the men are standing.

Opposite page - lower: **Leigh Road in the 1920s**. Compared with other views of the same area, this time Lewington's shop has gone whilst the wall of the Home Tavern is also windowless. During the 1960s the tobacconist's on the right was once owned by the author's uncle. Lloyd's bank is also prominent.

Above: **The Crescent – North-East side.** As the name implies, this road was built in the form of an arc and was recorded by the photographer probably sometime within the first three decades of the twentieth century.

Leigh Road (from Station) Eastleigh

Council Chambers, Leigh Rd, Eastleigh.

Willstred
Southampton.

WILLSTEED
SOUTHAMPTON.   THE COUNCIL OFFICES, EASTLEIGH.   404.

TOWN HALL, EASTLEIGH.   G 4061

CRANBURY ROAD, EASTLEIGH. 43.

Above: **Cranbury Road School.** A wonderful posed view of the children at this school; note especially the little girl with the hoop on the left. From the clothing the suggested date is during the Edwardian era. On the right the building with the porch was a Mission church and Parish hall. It was later used as 'Centre 66' but was finally destroyed by fire in 1989.

Opposite page: **The seat of Local Government**: The Leigh Road Council Chambers - better known as the Town Hall and offices, were originally built in 1898 but later extensively rebuilt and extended. In the lower view it will be noted that the surviving centre section has had a clock added to the original tower. Decades later the building remains basically unaltered, although it has for some years ceased to be used for its original function and is now a centre for arts and cultural events - known as The Point.

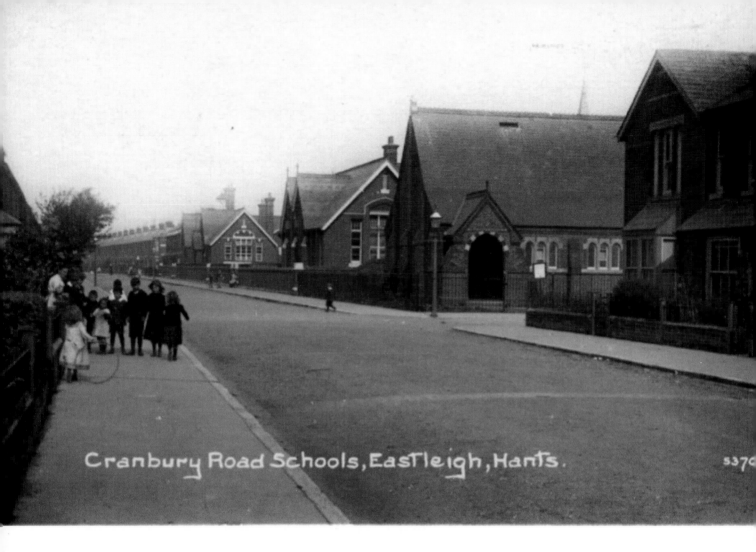

Cranbury Road Schools, Eastleigh, Hants.   5370

Above: **Within the Community**. With accommodation provided for the workers, the railway in association with the borough had also to cater for the needs of the workers' families. Unlike other towns, notably perhaps Swindon, community facilities such as schools and churches were not provided by the railway; instead this was the responsibility of the borough. One of the new schools provided was that in Cranbury Road, and much of the building is still in use for education today. The building on the right was later re-designated 'Centre 66' and, as previously noted, subsequently destroyed by fire.

Opposite page - top: **Grantham Road in the 1920s.** On the corner of Grantham Road was Gover's bakery, facing competition from the wall advert from T W Fry, Bakers and Grocers nearby. This same advert can still be discerned today.

Opposite page - lower: **Houses for the Workers -2.** Southampton Road at its intersection with Market Street and the location of the Eastleigh Hotel in the 'V' of the junction. The houses on the right of Southampton Road were demolished in the 1960s. One of their last uses was as refugee accommodation for what were believed to be 264 former residents from Tristan da Cunha all of whom had been evacuated in 1961 following a volcanic eruption. The islanders returned to their South Atlantic home two years later. The road sign advises motorists to 'Drive with Great Caution'.

Grantham Road, Eastleigh, Hants.   5344.

A 211 Eastleigh Hotel

Eastleigh Brotherhood Brass Band

This page - right: **Outings for the Workers - 1**. Another coach outing outside The Railway Institute. There would appear to be three AEC charabancs from 'Royal Blue'. The formal attire of the participants each with collar and tie is so typical of the men of the period even when off duty. Why the man to the left of centre is holding what appears to be a post-horn is not certain – unless to round up the travellers later on!

This page, centre and lower: **Outings for the Workers - 2 and 3**. Two views from a later outing and no doubt from the 1930s. The men are as smartly turned out as before although the vehicle operator this time is another local firm – Summerbee. The vehicles are though to be of Thorneycroft manufacture.

Opposite page - top: **An unknown note.** Unfortunately no information had been found on the Eastleigh Brotherhood Band as this book went to press. It was most likely a church orientated organisation as the white structure at the rear contains a young lady.

Opposite page - lower: **Coronation party**. A gathering of children outside the rebuilt Town Hall on the occasion of the Coronation of King George V1 in 1937. All are holding souvenir mugs presented to them on the occasion.

Leigh Road from the Station. An F.C.O. Stuart card of 1904, No 690 in the series, and with the photographer having briefly captured the attention of almost all the pedestrians visible. Notice in particular the apron-wearing worker from Prismall Bros and who has deliberately left his post in the shop so as to be included in the photograph. The premises of Prismall's later gave way to what is now the Nat West bank.

Station Hill. The intersection of three roadways, Station Hill, on which the pedestrians and carriages are located, with Bishopstoke Road to the right, and Southampton Road behind the photographer. Of the buildings at the bottom of the hill, only the former Church of The Resurrection which had been built in 1868 remains. After some time out of use, the interior was destroyed by fire in 1985, and although it has since been rebuilt, the Church is no longer a place of worship. Instead it was converted to a new use as housing association accommodation. The hilltop buildings are also survivors from the past, one being the Irish Club. These were erected between 1870 and 1881.

Station Hill, Eastleigh, Hants.

Surviving Public House. The 'Chamberlayne, basically unaltered to the present day. Built in 1887 it was witness to the start of the expansion of the location from a quiet Hampshire town to a major industrial community.
Railway Servants and Orphans Procession. Welfare support for those in need was limited in early years although it must be said that as an employer the railway company was better than most. Even so processions such as these – and probably dating from the very early 1900s - were intended to raise awareness of those less fortunate and hopefully secure donations. Indeed the wording appears to be something like: 'Feed my lambs'. The fire brigade are also followed by a military band.

Station Front – 1. An early view of the Station front recorded circa 1906 and from a retouched card. A group of horse drawn cabs are visible whilst it may also be noted that at this point in times past the tobacconist referred to earlier and located on the corner of Leigh Road was known by the name of W. Hall.

Smiles not Allowed. The Eastleigh and Bishopstoke Fire Brigade, smart and proud although unsmiling, for what was an official photograph. The group at the rear is seated on a horse drawn crew wagon which would have accompanied the actual fire engine to an incident.

Forerunners of the NatWest Bank. NatWest Bank was of course an amalgamation of the National Provincial and Westminster banks, and has occupied a site in Eastleigh opposite the railway station for many years. Prior to this though the site was in the hands of the Union and Smiths Bank, which had taken over the location from Prismall's stores. Next door was another butcher's, Messrs Budd's.

Marsh's Stores. The remains of Marsh's store after its destruction by fire on 8th May 1909. Previously this had been Butler's Ironmongers.

RICKET, MATCH, SUFFRAGETTES, V, POLICE, EASTLEIGH CARNIVAL 1907,

Above: **'Softly – Softly'** The location of the actual park here is uncertain although as described on the card itself the occasion was recorded as showing détente between the authorities and the suffragette movement in 1907. This was just one of a number of sports events held on the same day.

THE RECREATION GROUND, EASTLEIGH. 435

Above: Sunshine Day. Children and adults enjoying the sunshine in Leigh Road and the recreation ground. The view also makes for an interesting comparison with that seen in the snow from a similar location. Clearly from the Edwardian era, this is confirmed by the postmark of the card – August 1913.

Opposite page - lower: The Social Scene – 1. As mentioned at the start of the book, the railway town developed a number of community amenities for the workforce and their families, some of course provided by the railway and some by the local council. The cycle track in Dutton lane was an example, although its origins are not certain. The view is of a slow race about to start, assisted by convalescing soldiers from one of the First World War casualty clearing camps that were sited within the Eastleigh area.

Lower High Street, Eastle

Milk by the Jug. Another dairy operating from Eastleigh was that of Messrs Ivemy whose premises were located at 2 Doncaster Road. The view is of the High Street and with what could well be a gallon jug standing on the pavement – milk would be poured out into the customers' own receptacles as the milkman went from door to door. Notice also that this is a hand-operated cart although there is clear evidence of horse use of the roadway in the distance.

Hants.

5367.

Eastley Farmhouse. With its name taken from the original spelling of the Borough, this old building was demolished by Hampshire Constabulary in the 1950s to make way for a house for the local Police Superintendent.

Outdoor Bathing. The borough swimming pool situated in Bishopstoke Road and close to what was then Nutbeem Mill, later the site of the Mercedes dealership and more recently rebuilt as offices. As a schoolboy, I always remember the water as freezing cold – 'Good for the spirit', we were told. It certainly put me off swimming!

Borton Mill, Bishopstoke, Hants.

5335.

Nutbeem's Mill - 1. The building stood opposite the present day Chickenhall Lane with Barton Road visible on the right. It is possible to date the view as being from the First World War period due to the group of what were probably convalescing soldiers in Casualty Hospital uniform.

Nutbeem's Mill – 2. The rear of the Mill and with the Mill House on the right. On the left is Nutbeem Farm – now the site of the filling station on the corner of Chickenhall Lane. As an example of the changing times in the area, the author can clearly recall cattle in the front yard of the farm.

BARTON MILL EASTLEIGH.

Left: **Airport Bridge Complete.** The airport bridge in 1907/8 and supplementing the earlier view of the structure under construction in 1906. The view was taken almost from the position of the present roundabout leading to the motorway. On the left, the building was the original level crossing keeper's house which survived until 1966 and the opening of the airport station.

Above: **Bridges**. Erection of the skew girder road bridge over the railway at the south end of what is now Southampton Parkway station. Prior to this, Wide Lane crossed the railway at this point by a level crossing. In the background the former level crossing keeper's house remained in situ until the 1960s, when the airport and Parkway Station were built. Compared with other main lines, the LSWR route from Waterloo as far as Southampton West (Central) had few level crossings, with the only remaining one being at Mount Pleasant near St Denys.

Opposite page - top: **Early Days at the Airport**. Atlantic Park Hostel and after it had for a time been used by the US Naval Air Force. The site was first used for flying in 1918 by the USA after which it became a location for demobilising several RAF squadrons. Following this it was named as seen here and was taken over by a variety of shipping companies used to house European immigrants waiting for through passage to the Americas. For the time it was used as a hostel, flying was curtailed although Surrey Flying Services continued to operate a limited service of pleasure flights. Additionally the renowned R. J. Mitchell brought his 'Sparrow' design of aircraft to Eastleigh for a Government competition, and later of course the 'Spitfire' would make its first flight from Eastleigh.

ATLANTIC PARK HOSTEL, NEAR EASTLEIGH. 15.

Lower: **Station Front – 2.** The same scene, but some eight years later, and this time also with the first 'horseless' carriage in view. In the distance to the right, the arched notice of the Junction Hotel reads, 'Carriages for Hire & Livery Stables'. Notice the tobacconist's on the corner has by this time been demolished.

'Above: **Awayday'** - well not quite! Aside from housing the works of the Chief Mechanical Engineer or Locomotive Superintendent as the post was formally known, Eastleigh was also the home base to various groups of men in other departments who would have specific responsibility for their tasks over a wider area. The Eastleigh Bridge Gang for example had responsibility for the Meon Valley line as well, and are seen here involved in maintenance on the renowned West Meon viaduct.

The New Houses, Eastleigh.

Railway Houses – Dutton Lane. Located almost opposite the Carriage Works in Bishopstoke Road, Dutton Lane remains little altered to this day. For many years the LSWR Signal Department also had a depot accessed from this road. The cycle track and sports ground previously referred to were beyond the far end of this road.

Opposite page - lower: **Shakespeare Road from the Salisbury Line.** An expanding population in the 1920s and 1930s led to the need to develop more local authority housing within what was now the Borough of Eastleigh. One of the areas chosen was that of Shakespeare Road together with Arthur Road and The Quadrangle. Depicted here are new properties built, according to the card, by 'A Holloway –

Right: **The Junction Hotel.** Taking its name from both the railway and road junctions alongside, this was the hotel which once stood on the corner of Bishopstoke and Southampton Roads and in the place of where one of the station car-parks is now situated. Whilst no doubt a welcome retreat for the weary traveller, it cannot by any stretch of the imagination have been considered a quiet retreat.

The Junction Hotel, Eastleigh.

Bishopstoke Road Bridge. The bridge depicted was provided in 1890 and replaced a shorter, narrower construction described as being of 'slight' construction. It is thought there may even have been a level crossing on the site very early on. The town goods yard can also be seen

On the immediate left is the former town goods yard, nowadays the Lidl supermarket, the now demolished brick buildings against the road bridge formerly used by the railway Chief Civil Engineers department. At the time the view was taken in the 1960s, Station Hill was also one way, the road system meaning traffic was directed along Leigh Road and Upper Market Street to complete the circuit. Ford vehicles dominate the scene, a Consul Classic, Mk4 Zephyr, and Anglia visible, along with a Vauxhall, Triumph Herald, and the ubiquitous Morris 1000. In the railway yard though is a more select model of the period, a Rover Coupé.